The KnowHow Book of Action Games

CORWIN BOOKS

Sterling Publishing Co., Inc.
New York

Written and devised by:
Anne Civardi

Contributors:
James Opie, Andras Ranki
and Christopher Carey

Designed by:
John Jamieson
Illustrated by:
Malcolm English

This Sterling Publishing Co., Inc. edition
is published by arrangement with
Ottenheimer Publishers, Inc.

Sterling Publishing Co., Inc.
419 Park Avenue South, New York,
N.Y. 10016

Manufactured in the United States
of America

About This Book

This book shows you how to
make and play lots of different
kinds of games. There are
board games, dice games, table
games, races, battle games,
paper games and puzzles. Most
of the games are made from
things you can probably find at
home. There is a list on page 4
which tells you what things
you need and where to get them.

At the end of the book there
are six pages of party games,
party races and treasure hunts.

The measurements given are
only a guide. You can make the
games any size you like.

Remember to read the rules of
each game carefully so you
understand how to play them
before you begin.

The KnowHow Book of Action Games

Contents

4 Getting Ready
6 Beetle Bugs
7 Frog Leaps
8 There and Back
10 Looping the Loop
12 Five Minute Games
14 Mouse Trap
15 Fish Hook
16 Cannonboard
18 Flick Billiards
19 Tiddly Pong
20 Sticks and Kicks
22 Grand Derby
23 Crossing the Line

24 2-In-1 Board
26 Paper Games
28 Push and Shove
29 Jumpers
30 Skittle Scatter
32 Cops and Robbers
34 Picture Puzzles
36 Shotpot
38 Floor War
40 Space Mission
42 Party Games
44 Party Races
46 Treasure Hunts
48 Index

Getting Ready

These are the things you need to make the games in this book:

Thick cardboard - cut from strong cardboard boxes which you can get in supermarkets.
Thin cardboard - cut from empty cereal boxes, backs of writing pads, etc.
Glue - any all-purpose glue.
Sheet sponge - artificial sponge sold in sheets in craft and department stores.
Modeling clay - sold in toy stores.
Tiddly wink disks - flat, round plastic chips sold in packs in toy stores.
Checkers - wooden or plastic disks used to play checkers and sold in toy stores.
Doweling rods - wooden sticks sold in hardware stores.
Garden canes - sold in gardening shops.
Eye screws - sold in hardware stores.
Paint - use poster paint or water colors.
Tracing paper - use very thin, see-through paper.

Ask your friends to help you collect things like:
Various sizes of paper cups.
Cardboard tubes — from kitchen and toilet paper rolls.
Cardboard or plastic egg cartons.
Bag ties — used to tie up freezer and garbage bags.
Cardboard boxes in different sizes.
Thin and thick cardboard.
Empty plastic squeeze bottles.
Corks, empty matchboxes, hairpins, pipe cleaners, and marbles.

Homemade Boxes

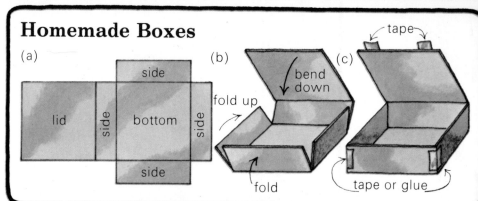

If you cannot find a box, make one out of cardboard. Use a ruler to draw the lines. The lid and bottom are the same size and the sides are all the same size (a).

Fold the cardboard, like this, to make the lid, bottom and sides (b). Stick the sides together with glue or tape (c). Try making a box without a lid.

1 Who Begins?

There are lots of ways to choose the starter of a game. One is for all the players to throw dice. The one with the highest number starts (a). Play clockwise from the starter.

Another way is to draw straws. Each player picks one. The one with the longest straw starts (b). Or cut up slips of paper. Draw an X on one.

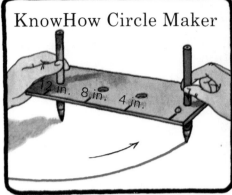

KnowHow Circle Maker

Measure and punch holes every 4 in. on a strip of thin cardboard, like this. Stick pencils through two holes. Holding both pencils firmly, swing one around in a circle.

Cardboard Dice

(a) ¾ in. ¾ in. ¾ in. ¾ in.

(b) glue glue glue

To make cardboard dice, draw this shape, with all the sides ¾ in. long, on some thin cardboard. Paint the dots in each square, like this (a).

Fold in along the lines and glue the sides and the top together (b). On dice the two sides opposite each other always add up to seven.

Clay and Sugar Dice

(a) (b)

clay   sugar cube

To make a die, shape a lump of modeling clay into a cube and mark in the dots with a pencil point, like this (a). You can also ink dots on a sugar cube to make a die (b).

(c) (d)

Fold them in half and jumble them up. Everyone takes a slip. The player with the X starts (c). When there are only two players, toss a coin to see who starts (d).

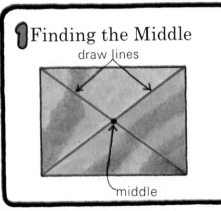

Finding the Middle

draw lines

middle

To find the middle of a box, a piece of cardboard or a sheet of paper, draw lines across it from the four corners, like this. The middle is where the lines cross.

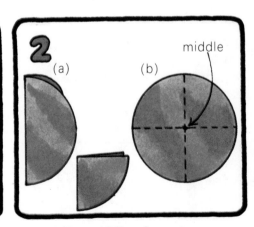

middle

(a) (b)

To find the middle of a paper or thin cardboard circle, fold it in half twice, like this (a). Open the circle out again. The middle is where the two folds cross (b).

Beetle Bugs
(for 2 or more players)

Make enough Beetle Bug parts to build a complete Bug for each player. If you do not have any modeling clay, try using clean potatoes for the head and body.

You will need
a die and a small container for a
  dice shaker

For each Beetle Bug
modeling clay or 2 potatoes
a toothpick or matchstick and
  some aluminum foil
2 paper fasteners
thin wire (about 4 in. long)
tissue paper, a pencil and
  some strong glue
6 used wooden matchsticks or
  toothpicks

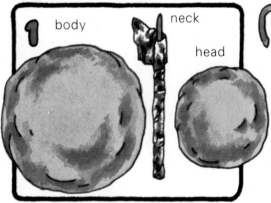

Shape two lumps of modeling clay into a round body and a smaller round head. Wrap aluminum foil around a toothpick or used matchstick to make the neck.

To make a curly tongue, wrap a strip of tissue paper around the thin wire. Glue the paper at both ends (a). Twist the wire around a pencil, like this (b), and slide it off (c).

How to Play

The idea is to build a complete Bug by throwing the die for each part of the body. Each number on the die matches a part of the body. If you throw a number you do not need, wait until your next turn.

To start, each player must throw a 1 for the body. Then throw a 2 for the neck or a 6 for each leg. When he has the neck, he throws for the head and the eyes and tongue. The winner is the first player to make up a Beetle Bug with a body, neck, a head, 2 eyes, a tongue and 6 legs.

Numbers to Throw

body	⚀
neck	⚁
head	⚂
eye	⚃
tongue	⚄
leg	⚅

Frog Leaps

(for 2 or more players)

This is a frog race. Each player needs a cardboard frog. The frogs start at one end of the strings and jump along to the other. The finishing line can be a mark on the floor or ponds made out of cardboard for the frogs to jump into.

You will need

thick cardboard
a piece of string (about 6 ft. long) for each player
tracing paper
a pencil and some paint
scissors
thin cardboard to make the cardboard ponds

How to Play

(a) upright
(b) half down
(c) half up
cardboard pond

Fasten one end of each string to a chair leg so the frogs stand in a line with their feet just touching the floor. Put a cardboard pond at the other end of each string.

Each player holds the end of a string and jerks it up and down to make the frog leap along it. The first frog to get into its pond or past the finishing line wins.

1

draw (a)
scribble (b)
(c) draw
cardboard

Trace this frog pattern on tracing paper (a). Turn the paper over and scribble over the back (b). Put it, right side up, on the cardboard and draw around the pattern again (c).

2

hole

Cut out the frog shape. Paint it a bright color with big eyes and a mouth. Make a hole in the middle of the body where the mark is and thread string through it.

Frog Pattern

There and Back

(for 2, 3 or 4 players)

This is the great bicycle race all the way to Chiromo Village and back. Play the game on this board.

How to Play

Each player needs a cardboard bicycle, made as shown below. The first player to race his bicycle from the Cycle Park to Chiromo Village and back to the Cycle Park is the winner. Players take their bikes with them when they go by air or sea.

To start, each player puts his bicycle on one of the squares in the Cycle Park. Everyone throws the dice. The player with the highest number begins by moving his bicycle the number of points on the dice. When two bicycles land on the same square, those two players must shout, "give way." The last one to shout the words loses his next turn.

Players must take different routes from each other when they go by air or sea. Some routes are faster than others. The supersonic jet is faster than the balloon and the ocean liner is faster than the row boat.

Making the Bicycles

bend forward   cut   bend back

To make a bicycle, trace the pattern onto some cardboard and cut the shape out. Paint the bicycle a different color for each player.

Looping the Loop

(for 2 or more players)

This is a target board. The further you stand from the board, the harder it is to get the rings around the pegs.

You will need
a big cardboard box lid (about 11 in. wide and 16 in. long)
colored paper or paint
5 cardboard tubes cut from a kitchen roll, or thin cardboard
thick cardboard
strong glue and string
scissors and a pencil

cover or paint lid

cardboard tubes

To make the board, cover a cardboard box lid with colored paper, or paint the outside and leave it to dry.

Make five cardboard pegs out of cardboard tubes, like this. The longest should be about 5 in. long and the shortest about 3 in. long, as shown.

glue

Glue the pegs, slanting upward, to the outside of the lid. Put the shortest one in the middle and the others close to the four corners, like this.

paint

When the pegs are firmly stuck to the lid, paint them all different colors. Leave them to dry.

make hole

1 in.

Turn the board on one side and make a hole about 1 in. from the top, like this. Do the same on the other side. Thread a piece of string through the holes. Knot the ends.

Draw ten circles on a sheet of thick cardboard, using the bottom of a can or coffee jar lid as a guide. Make sure the circles are at least twice as wide as the pegs.

Using a lightly smaller lid or can, draw a circle inside each big circle, like this. Cut around the big circles and then cut out the middle circles.

paint

Glue two circles together to make a thick cardboard ring. Do this with all the circles so that you have five rings. Paint each ring the same color as one of the pegs.

2

5 in.

5 in.

(a)

(b)

fold around

tape or glue

(c)

If you do not have any old cardboard tubes, make the pegs out of thin cardboard. Cut five pieces of cardboard, each about 5 in. wide and 5 in. long (a).

Curl each piece around your finger (b) and tape or glue the two edges together (c). Cut them so they are all slightly different lengths.

3

cut

Cut one end of each tube at an angle, like this. This is to make them slant upward when you glue them onto the cardboard box lid.

7

2 5
10
4 1

Cut out five small squares of white paper. Glue one square below each of the colored pegs. Draw or paint the numbers shown on the squares.

How to Play

Hang the board on a door. Place a string on the floor about 6 ft. from the board. Stand behind the string and try to throw the rings onto the pegs. Throw the five colored rings in one turn.

If you step over the line while throwing, miss a turn. When a ring lands around a peg, score the number of points marked under the peg. If a ring lands around the same colored peg, score twice the number. The first to score 50 points wins.

Five Minute Games

(for lots of players)

The games on these two pages are very easy to make and only take a few minutes to play.

You will need
For Egg Flip
2 cardboard 6-egg cartons and a fork
For Catchball
2 tall plastic cups
a table tennis ball
8 rubber bands
thin and thick cardboard
For Blow Football
2 small cardboard boxes
modeling clay and 2 straws
a table tennis ball
For Ribbon Roll
1 tall, plastic cup
5 small paper cups
ribbon (about 1 in. wide and 1 yd. long)
a pin
thick cardboard and white paper
5 marbles
For Matchbox Bullseye
thin cardboard and a matchbox
For all the games
paint, glue, scissors, a pencil and transparent tape

1 Egg Flip

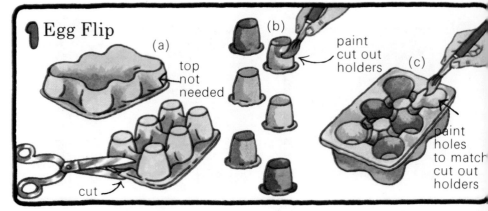

Cut the tops off both egg cartons and throw them away. Cut the six egg holders out of the bottom of one egg carton (a). Paint each egg holder a different color (b). Let it dry.

Paint the six holes in the bottom of the second egg carton. Make them the same colors as the egg holders, like this (c).

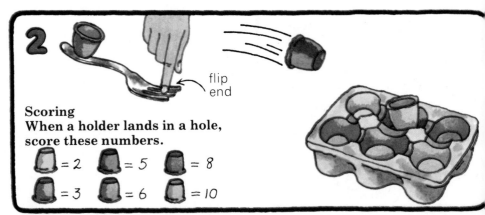

Scoring
When a holder lands in a hole, score these numbers.

= 2   = 5   = 8
= 3   = 6   = 10

Put the painted egg carton bottom on the floor. Put a fork about 18 in. from the carton, like this. To play, balance an egg holder, open end up, on the handle end of the fork.

Push down quickly on the prongs and try to flip the holder into a hole in the egg carton. Mark down the score. A holder that lands in the same colored hole scores double.

1 Catchball

Draw two circles on cardboard, using the bottom of a plastic cup (a). Cut them out ¼ in. smaller all the way around. Now cut off the bottom of the cup (b).

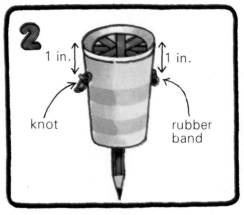

Make a catcher in the same way as you would make a cannon (see page 17). Instead of a cardboard tube, use the plastic cup and the circles you have cut out.

Cut out a strip of thin cardboard, about 9 in. wide and 4 in. long. Glue it around the bottom of the plastic cup catcher, like this. Now make another catcher.

1 Blow Football

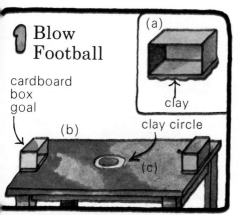

cardboard box goal

(a)

clay

clay circle

(b)

(c)

Put some modeling clay on the bottom of two small cardboard boxes (a). Push them, clay side down, onto the ends of a table (b). Put a clay circle in the middle (c).

2

Two people, or four people playing in teams of two, can play. To start, put a table tennis ball in the clay circle in the middle of the table, like this.

The players each have a straw and stand on either side of the table. The idea is to blow the ball, using the straws, into the other team's goal.

1 Ribbon Roll

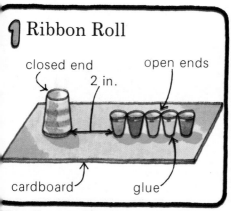

closed end

open ends

2 in.

cardboard

glue

Glue five small paper cups, open ends up and touching each other, to cardboard. Glue a tall, plastic cup, open end down, about 2 in. from the first cup, like this.

2

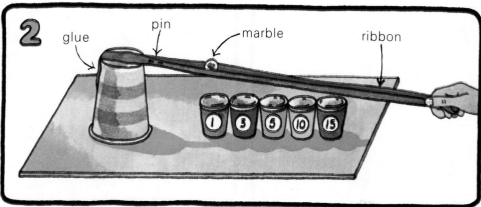

glue

pin

marble

ribbon

1 3 5 10 15

Glue one end of some ribbon, about 1 in. wide and 1 yd. long, to the top of the large cup. Pin the ribbon together close to the cup like this, so that it funnels.

Draw these numbers on pieces of paper. Glue them onto the pots. Roll marbles, one by one, down the ribbon and try to get them into the cups. Roll five marbles in each turn.

4

pull

Stand 9 ft. apart. Each player holds a catcher. The game is to fire and catch a table tennis ball, using the catchers. The player to catch the ball five times in a row wins.

Matchbox Bullseye

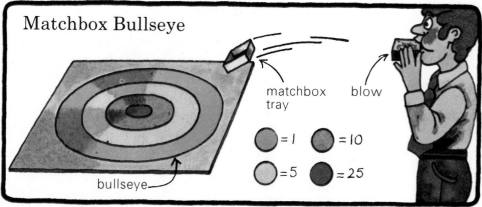

matchbox tray

blow

bullseye

🔴 = 1   🔴 = 10
🔴 = 5   🔴 = 25

Draw a big circle on some cardboard. Draw three smaller circles inside it, like this. Paint them all different colors. When they are dry paint on the numbers.

Stand 6 ft. from the board. Put a matchbox in your mouth and blow hard so that the match tray shoots out onto the colored circles. Have three blows in each turn.

Mouse Trap

(for 3 or more players)

Each player needs a cork mouse.
Instead of making a spinner you
can play with dice.

You will need
a cork for each player
pieces of string (each about
    16 in. long)
a hairpin and felt cloth
scissors and strong glue
a plastic container or
    little box
thin cardboard
a used wooden matchstick or a
    toothpick
tracing paper and a pencil
paint and a paintbrush
a circle of cardboard for the
    cardboard mat

1 Mouse Making

push down

Paint the corks different colors.
Leave them to dry. Then make a
hole through the middle of each
cork, using closed scissors or a
knitting needle, like this.

2

(a)

double-knot

(b)

Loop string, about 16 in. long,
around a hairpin (a). Push the
hairpin through the hole in a cork
and double knot the end of the string
(b). Do the same to all the corks.

3

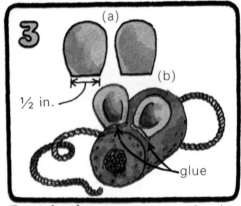

(a)

(b)

½ in.

glue

To make the mouse ears, cut out
two pieces of felt this shape (a).
Glue them to the top of the cork,
like this (b). Put two ears on all the
cork mice.

Spinner

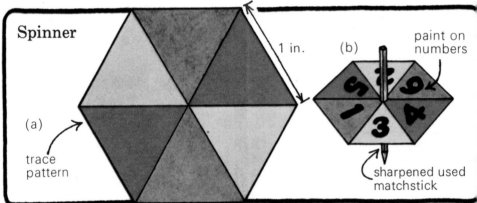

(a)

1 in.

(b)

paint on
numbers

trace
pattern

sharpened used
matchstick

Trace this pattern (a) onto thin
cardboard. Draw lines from corner
to corner, like this. Cut the shape
out very carefully.

Paint the triangles and paint on the
numbers. Sharpen a used match
with a pencil sharpener. Push it
through the middle of the spinner,
where all the lines meet, or use a
toothpick.

How to Play

plastic
container

cardboard
mat

Players spin the spinner in turn.
The one with the highest number is
the mouse trapper. The others are
the mouse holders. Each holder puts
his mouse on the cardboard mat and
holds its tail. The trapper spins the
spinner. When it stops on a 6 or 4 he
tries to trap the mice under the
container. The holders try to pull
them away before being trapped. If
the trapper catches a mouse he
scores 5 points. A holder scores 5
points if he pulls his mouse away in
time.

A holder loses 5 points if he pulls his
mouse away when the spinner stops
on a number other than a 6 or 4. The
first player to score 50 points wins.

When the trapper has spun a 6 or 4
three times, he passes the container
to the player on his left who then
becomes the new mouse trapper.

Fish Hook

(for 2 or more players)

This is a race against time. Try to hook as many cork fish as you can before all the salt runs out of the timer.

You will need
- corks
- eye screws or hairpins
- some felt cloth
- strong glue and white paper
- a stick (about 20 in. long)
- string
- a hairpin or thin wire
- scissors and paint
- a plastic squeeze bottle
- a glass jar
- salt or fine sand

How to Play

Put the fish, screw ends up, on the floor. Take turns to hook the fish with the rod. Add up the numbers on the fish you have hooked after each turn.

A turn lasts as long as it takes for the salt to pour out of the squeeze bottle, once the lid has been opened. The first player to score 20 points wins.

1 Fish Making

eye screw

bent hairpin

Paint six corks different colors. Screw an eye screw into the middle of the small end of each cork, or push a hairpin into the cork, like this.

2

(a)

half-way around cork

glue on cloth

(b)

paint on eyes

Cut two pieces of felt, each wide enough to wrap halfway around a cork (a). Glue the felt onto the cork and paint on eyes, like this (b). Do the same to all six corks.

3

glue on numbers

Cut out six circles of white paper and glue one to the bottom of each cork. Paint numbers from one to six on the paper, like this.

4

rod or stick

(b)

tie on string

(a)

bent hairpin hook

attach hook

Tie string, about 23 in. long, to one end of a stick or rod. Bend a hairpin or some wire into a hook, like this (a) and tie it onto the end of the string (b).

5 KnowHow Timer

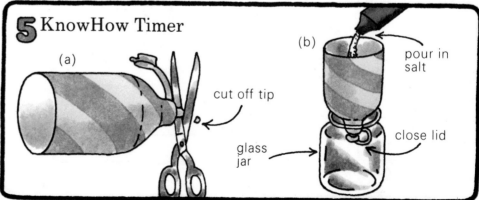

(a)

cut off tip

glass jar

(b)

pour in salt

close lid

Cut a squeeze bottle in half. Cut off the very tip of the bottle, like this (a). Paint the bottle with brightly colored paint. Let it dry.

Close the lid and balance the squeeze bottle, upside down, in a glass jar. Fill the bottle with salt or fine sand (b), making sure there are no lumps in it.

Cannonboard
(for 2 or more players)

The further you pull the pencil out of the cannon, the faster the marbles will go. Pull it very gently to get marbles into the goals nearest the cannon.

You will need

a strong cardboard box (about 14 in. wide and 18 in. long)
a sheet of thin cardboard
a strong cardboard tube (about 6 in. long)
4 rubber bands
6 marbles
transparent tape and strong glue
a pencil, a ruler and scissors

How to Play

Fire the marbles out of the cannon and try to get them into the goals with the high numbers. Each player fires six marbles in each turn. At the end of each turn add up the plus scores and take away the minus scores. The first player to score 100 points wins.

To fire, put one marble at a time into the top of the cannon. Pull back the pencil and then let it go.

1 The Board

bend forward — strip

cut slits

glue

cut open flap

Cut a flap, about 2 in. wide, at one corner of the box. Cut a strip of cardboard half the length of the box and as high. Cut slits on one side. Glue the strip to the box.

2

glue on strip

Cut a strip of cardboard about 1½ times the width of the box and as high. Cut slits at both ends. Bend the strip into a half-circle and glue it to the sides of the box.

3

glue on goals

To make the goals, cut 13 pieces of cardboard, about 3 in. long and 1 in. wide. Cut slits at one edge of each piece. Bend them into half-circles. Glue them onto the box.

16

4
(a) bend
1½ in. (b)
1 in.
glue

ut out eight strips of cardboard, bout 1½ in. x 1 in. Cut slits along e edge of each strip, like this (a). oll them into small posts and glue em, as shown (b).

Now glue the posts onto the box, like this. They are hazards and make the game a bit harder to play. Draw or paint the plus and minus numbers inside each goal.

5
1½ times width
bend
fold on line
glue
glue

Cut some cardboard about 1½ times the width of the box and about 2 in. high. Cut slits along the edge. Bend the cardboard on the red lines. Glue it to one end of the back of the box, so that the box tilts from top to bottom.

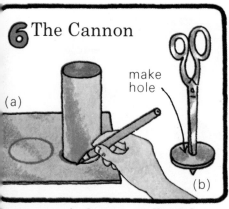

6 The Cannon
(a)
make hole
(b)

raw two circles on cardboard, sing the end of the cardboard tube). Cut them out, ¼ in. smaller all e way around. Glue together. ake a hole in the middle (b).

7
stick tape around circle and wrap around pencil
tape

Push the end of a pencil through the hole in the cardboard circle. Tape the circle onto the pencil very firmly, like this.

8
loop through and pull
make hole
1 in.
(a)
(b)

Link four strong rubber bands together, like this (a). Make a hole on either side of the tube, about 1 in. from one end (b).

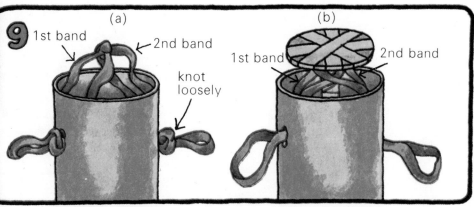

9
(a)
1st band
2nd band
knot loosely
(b)
1st band
2nd band

hread the rubber bands through e holes in the cardboard tube, ke this. Knot both ends very osely (a).

Push the cardboard circle and pencil up the tube. First pull one rubber band over the circle and then the other, like this. Untie the loose knots (b).

10 Cannon Mounting
¾ in.
-3 -2

Make a hole halfway up the two pieces of cardboard, about ¾ in. from the open flap. Push the rubber band ends through the holes, like this. Double knot each end.

Flick Billiards

(for 2 players or 2 teams)

To play this game, one player or team needs ten checkers of one color. The other player or team needs ten checkers of a different color. Glue a circle of white paper to the top of an extra checker. We have used black and red checkers.

You will need

a cardboard box with low sides
  (about 28 in. x 20 in.)
4 old nylon stockings
21 checkers
a small paper cup
thin cardboard
transparent tape and strong glue
scissors and a pencil

Draw a circle in each corner on the inside of the box, using a small paper cup as a guide. Cut out the four circles.

To make the corner nets, cut the feet off four old stockings. Glue one foot over each hole on the back of the box, like this.

To make a finger guard, cut a strip of thin cardboard. Put it over the nail of your third finger. Wrap transparent tape around it, like this. The picture shows you how to flick.

How to Play

The player with the black checkers starts. He flicks a black checker against a red one, trying to get the red one into a corner net. If he does, he has another turn. If not, the player with the red checkers tries to flick a black one into a net. If either player flicks the extra checker into a net, he picks one of his checkers and the extra one out of the net and puts them back on the board. The first one to flick all the other side's checkers into the nets wins.

This picture shows where to place the checkers at the start of the game.

Tiddly Pong

(for 2 players)

This is just like ordinary table tennis except that you can play on a small table. Both players need a bat to hit the ball over the net to each other.

You will need

a sheet of thick cardboard
thin cardboard
a sheet of sponge
a saucer
an old nylon stocking
a table tennis ball
strong glue and transparent tape
scissors and string
a safety pin and 4 pencils

(a) cardboard / saucer

(b) glue bat shapes together

Draw two lines, 1½ in. apart and 4 in. long, on thick cardboard. Draw a circle at the bottom of the lines, using a saucer. Cut out the shapes. Glue them together. Do this again.

(a) sheet sponge / tape

(b) glue on sponge

Using the same saucer, draw four circles on a sheet of sponge (a). Cut them out. Glue a sponge circle to both sides of a cardboard bat, like this (b).

tape / string / push pencil up

Wrap string tightly around the handle of each bat. Glue the ends and wrap transparent tape around them. Push a pencil up the handles, between the two pieces of cardboard.

(a) stocking

(b) glue edges

To make the net, cut the foot off an old stocking. Cut open the stocking, like this (a). Fold over and glue about ¾ in. at both edges, as shown (b).

safety pin (a)

(b) pencils

Cut two pieces of string 31 in. long. Loop them, one at a time, through a closed safety pin (a). Thread them through the folded stocking (b). Tie the ends to two pencils.

thin cardboard / 2 in.

tape / table

Cut two pieces of thin cardboard as long as the lip on the table you use and about 2 in. wide. Tape one to the middle of each side of the table. Push the pencils into them.

How to Play

The aim is to be the first to score 21 points. You score a point when the other player cannot return your shot. Take turns serving.

Each player has 5 serves in a turn. The ball must bounce on both sides of the table when you serve. It must not bounce on your side when you return a shot.

Sticks and Kicks

(for 2 players)

You will need

a strong cardboard box (about
   18 in. long, 10 in. wide and 3 in.
   deep)
thick cardboard
a cardboard egg carton
a strong cardboard tube (from a
   paper towel roll)
2 small string bags or a stocking
4 garden canes or 4 thin sticks
   (each about 24 in. long)
modeling clay and 4 corks
4 big rubber bands
a pencil and paint
a small ball or large marble

How to Play

**Put the box on a table. Put the ball
or marble inside the circle on the
center line. Players stand on
different sides of the table and
hold a rod in each hand. Both
start together.**

**The idea is to twist, push and pull
the canes and try to get your
football players to kick the ball
into the other team's goal. The
first team to score three goals is
the winner.**

1 glue on strips

glue in
cardboard

Cut some cardboard the size of the
bottom of the box. Glue it inside
the box, like this. Glue strips of
cardboard to the sides and ends of
the box, too.

2 paint

flap
3 in.
wide

Cut a flap, about 3 in. wide, at both
ends of the box, like this. Then paint
the cardboard glued inside the box.
Let it dry.

3 decorate sides

goal
circle

center

Draw a line across the middle of the
inside of the box. Draw a circle on
the line, like this, using a cup as a
guide. Draw half-circles around the
goal flaps.

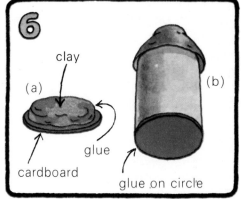

To make a goal net, cut open a string vegetable bag or use a piece of stocking (a). Put one edge under the goal flap. Glue it underneath the box. Glue the other edge to the sides and top of the box (b).

To make the football players, cut the paper towel roll into six tubes, each 2 in. long. Cut six egg holders out of the egg carton. Glue one holder to the top of each tube.

Draw around the bottom of each tube on cardboard. Cut out the circles. Glue modeling clay to each one (a). Glue a circle, clay inside, to the bottom of each tube.

Paint faces on all the cardboard tubes. Paint three football players one team color and the other three a different team color.

Measure the length of the sides of the box. Divide it in half to find the center. Draw lines at the center on both sides of the box, like this.

Make holes 2 in. from both sides of the center lines and 1¾ in. from the bottom of the box. Make holes 2 in. from both ends and 1¾ in. from the bottom of the box, as shown.

Push the canes through the holes in the box. Make holes in each tube (a). Push one team onto the canes at one end and the other team onto the canes at the other end (b).

Push each cane through the second hole. Wrap a rubber band around the end of each cane, like this, to stop them from getting pulled back through the holes.

Push corks onto the other ends to make handles. Pull the rods so that the rubber bands are against the box sides. Then glue the football players to the canes in position, like this.

Grand Derby

(for 2 or more players)

This is a horse race which you can play on any big table. Each player needs a horse and a jockey, and a piece of string long enough to loop around the table.

You will need
thin cardboard
tracing paper
a pencil and paint
string and scissors
strong glue
modeling clay
wire bag ties, pipe cleaners or
   thin wire

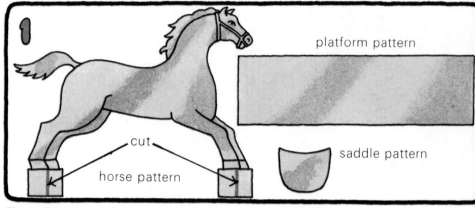

platform pattern

saddle pattern

cut

horse pattern

To make a horse, draw the horse pattern, saddle pattern and platform pattern on tracing paper. Then trace the patterns onto some thin cardboard.

Cut the horse, saddle and platform shapes out of the cardboard. Cut along the red lines on the horse's hoofs. Paint the shapes and let them dry.

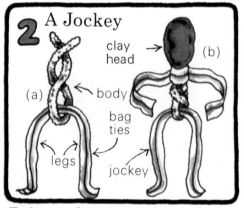

2 A Jockey

clay head

(a)

body

bag ties

legs

jockey

(b)

Twist two bag ties or pieces of wire together for the legs and body (a). Twist another one around the body to make arms. Push a clay head on the body (b).

3

knot

clay jumps

string looped around table

Loop as many pieces of string as there are players around a table. Knot the ends. Press pieces of clay down on the table under the strings, to make jumps.

4

glue

string

glue

platform

Glue a saddle onto the back of each horse. Put a horse over each string. Pull the string up the slits on the horses' hoofs. Bend the slits, as in the picture. Glue them to a platform.

How to Play

The game is to race your horse from one end of the table to the other without letting the jockey fall off. The horses must go over the jumps on the way. Anybody whose jockey falls off goes back to the beginning.

To start, put jockeys on the saddles. Line the horses at the start. Stand at that end of the table and pull the string under the table toward you. The first player to get his horse and jockey to the other end wins.

Start

Crossing the Line
(for 2 players)

Practice pushing the coin onto the board. Put it on the edge of the board and hit it with the palm of your hand so that it slides onto a colored strip.

You will need

thick cardboard (about 12 in. wide and 13 in. long)
thin cardboard
a ruler and a pencil
plastic wrap and strong glue
paint and a paintbrush
coins

Draw a rectangle, 11 in. wide and 12 in. long, on a piece of thick cardboard. Draw lines down the middle of the rectangle and 2 in. from either side, like this.

Draw nine lines 1¼ in. apart, across the rectangle. Rub out the fifth line so that you have one 2½ in. strip. Paint the seven middle strips different colors, like this.

Draw two circles on each side of the colored strips, except the middle strip, using a small coin. Paint the circles the same colors as the strips. Cover the board with plastic wrap.

Using the same coin, draw 24 circles on thin cardboard (a). Cut them out. Paint four circles the same color as each of the strips, except the middle strip (b).

How to Play

Put the board on a table. Lay a book behind it to keep it steady. Both players have a coin and 12 cardboard circles (2 of each color). One person plays on the left half of the board, the other on the right half.

Start with the coins on the white strip closest to you. Each player, in turn, pushes the coins onto the board. Each time the coin lands inside a colored strip, cover one of the circles beside it with the same color cardboard circle. If it lands on a line, wait for your next turn. If the coin lands on the middle strip, you lose a turn. The first one to cover all 12 circles on his side wins.

2-In-1 Board

1. Matchmake

(for 2 or 3 players)

You will need

red, blue and green modeling clay
used wooden matches and thumb tacks
a die and a board like this ———→

1 (a) clay (b) half a match
thumb tack

For the matchmen, push a small ball of clay onto a thumb tack (a). Push half a match into the clay (b). Make 14 red men, 14 blue men and 14 green men.

2 match-men

To set up the board, put the blue men on the dark blue squares, like this. Put the red men on the dark red squares and the green men on the dark green squares.

How to Play Matchmake

The game is to get your matchmen from the dark squares to the lighter squares of the same color with stars. Each player has 14 men of one color. Men can be moved in any direction except diagonally. Throw the die to start. Then take turns.

Each turn move one man the number on the die. You can capture an enemy man by landing on its square if it is not on its own color. Take any captured men off the board and keep them. You cannot jump over men.

The game ends when one player has moved all his remaining men on the board onto his star squares. To score, each player counts his men on the star squares, adds the number of men he has captured and takes away his men not on star squares. The player with the highest score wins.

2. Hop Over (for 2 players)

You will need
12 green matchmen and 12 red
   matchmen (see Matchmake)
1 die

How to Play Hop Over

Red
Home
Row

Red
Starting
Row

Green
Starting
Row

Green
Home
Row

To start, put 4 green matchmen on
the pink star squares in the corner
of the board, like this. Put 4 red
matchmen on the red squares in the
opposite corner. One player moves
the green men, the other the red men.

The game is to get your 12 matchmen
from their Starting Row to their
Home Row. Throw the dice in turn.
Move one man each turn according
to the number you throw. You must
move a man if possible. Each time a
man is moved out of a Starting Row
square put on a new man. Take off
any man who reaches its Home Row.

Men can move sideways along the row
they are on but only in one direction
each turn. If they cannot go the full
distance, they cannot move. Men
can jump over their own men. Up
to 3 men can be on the same square.

A 6 on the dice can be used to move
any one man forward to its next row,
like this. This is a Hop Over.

Green
Hop Over
Move

Red
Hop Over
Move

A 5 may be used for a Hop Over from
a square with 2 or 3 men on it. A 4
may be used for a Hop Over from a
square with 3 men on it.

A man can only Hop Over one enemy
man if there are 2 or 3 men on the square
it is hopping from. A man can Hop Over
2 enemy men if there are 3 men on the
square it is hopping from. The first
player to get all 12 of its matchmen
Home wins, or end the game when 6
men reach Home.

Paper Games
(for lots of players)

Jumbled Newspapers

Each player has a jumbled up newspaper with the pages out of order, upside down and wrongly folded. Everyone starts together. The first player to put all the pages of his paper back into the right order wins.

Animals of Four

Players sit in a circle, each with a pencil and a slip of paper. They write the name of an animal across the top of the paper, fold it over so it cannot be seen and pass it to the player on their left. On the slip they have been given they write the name of another animal, fold it over and pass it on. They do this four times. All the slips are put in the middle of the circle. Each player takes one. He draws a creature made up of the four animals written on his slip.

Noise Maker

One player is the noise maker. He collects ten things that make different noises. The other players each have a pencil and some paper. They sit in a room, close to a slightly open door. The noise maker stands behind the door. He shouts "number one" and then makes his first noise by, perhaps breaking a hard biscuit.

The players write down what they think the noise is. The noise maker then shouts "number two" and makes his next noise, perhaps rolling marbles inside a can. The players write down what they think it is. The player who has guessed the most noises correctly after the noise maker has made his ten noises wins.

Paper Hats

Each player has a big sheet of paper and some transparent tape. He has to make a hat out of the paper and put it on his head. The player who makes the best hat in three minutes wins.

Hangman

One player is the executioner. The other is the convict. The executioner thinks of a 6 or 7 letter word and marks down a dash for each letter on some paper. The convict tries to guess, one by one, the letters that make up the word.

For each wrong guess, the executioner draws in another part of the gallows and the hanging man. First the gallows, then the rope, then the head, the face, the body, the left arm, the right arm, the left leg and the right leg. If the convict guesses a letter in the word, the executioner writes it in position on the dash. If the convict guesses the whole word before he is hanged, he wins. If not, the executioner wins.

Team Drawing

One player is the boss. The others split into two teams. Each has some paper and a pencil. The boss writes down ten things to draw, such as "Tightrope walker," "ringing telephone" or "Olympics."

The teams stand at opposite ends of the room with the boss in the middle. The first player in each team runs to the boss who tells them both to draw the first thing on his list. They run back and draw it in front of their teams. When the team has guessed what it is the second player runs to the boss for his drawing. The first team to guess all ten drawings wins.

Keep on Folding

Each player has one page of a newspaper. While music plays, everyone hops about. When it stops, everyone quickly folds his newspaper in half and stands on it. The last person to stand on his paper is out. The music starts again. When it stops the players fold their papers in half again and stand on them. This goes on until the papers have been folded into tiny squares and there is only one player left. He wins the game.

Drawing Blind

Players are blindfolded. Each has some paper and a pencil. They are told to draw a picture, such as a boat race, bit by bit. First they draw the sea, then the boats, then a lighthouse, the sky and the clouds. The blindfolds are taken off and the player who has drawn the best picture is given a prize.

Battleships

This is a game for two. Both players draw two big squares on some paper and draw nine lines across and down them, as shown. Along the top of each big square they write numbers from 1 to 10. Down the side they write letters from A to J. One big square is the Battle Area, the other is the Target Area. Without letting each other see where, the players draw ten battleships on their Battle Areas. Five battleships cover two squares each and five cover one square each. The ships must not touch.

Players must not let each other see their papers during the game. Each player takes a turn to attack. Each turn a player calls out a number and a letter, such as A6. If the other player has a whole ship on that square, he says "hit." The attacker marks a B on his Target Area. If part of a ship is on that square, the defender says "touched." The attacker knows he has only sunk half a ship. If no ship is on that square, the attacker draws an X in the same square on his Target Area. Then the other player is the attacker. The winner is the first one to sink all the other player's battleships.

Push and Shove

(for 2 players or 2 teams)

For this board game, one player or team needs ten checkers of one color, the other needs ten of a different color. The bigger you make the board, the more fun it is to play. Flick enemy checkers off high scoring circles.

You will need

a big, square sheet of thick
    cardboard (about 25 in. long
    and 25 in. wide)
thin cardboard
a KnowHow circle maker (see
    page 5)
strong glue and scissors
paint and paintbrush
20 checkers and a finger guard (see page 18)

Make a KnowHow circle maker (see page 5). Punch a hole above the 0 mark, 4 in. mark, 8 in. mark and the 12 in. mark, like this.

Find the middle (see page 5) of the square sheet of cardboard. Draw three circles, like this, using the 4 in., 8 in. and 12 in. holes of the circle maker.

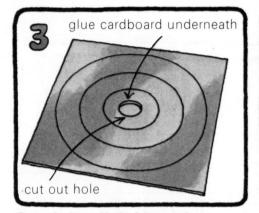

Cut a hole, a little bigger than a checker, out of the center of the board. Glue a square of cardboard underneath the hole. Then paint the circles different colors.

Cut out eight pieces of cardboard, each about 3 in. x 1 in. Make cuts along one edge of each piece (a). Roll them into posts (b). Glue the ends and bend out the cuts (c).

Glue the posts, at equal distances, around the edge of the inside circle, like this. The space between two posts should be big enough for a checker to go through.

How to Play

When two people play, each has 10 checkers. If four play, in teams of two, each has 5. Partners use the same color and sit opposite each other.

Take turns to flick the checkers, one by one. Try to get them on to the high scoring circles. If a checker lands on a line, count the lower score. Try to flick them behind posts to stop being hit. The player or team with the highest score after all 20 checkers have been flicked wins.

= 5 (outer circle)

= 10 (middle circle)

= 15 (inner circle)

= 25 (hole)

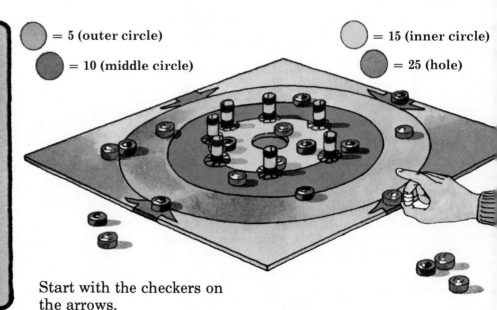

Start with the checkers on the arrows.

Jumpers

(for 2 or more players)

This is a different sort of tiddly winks. Try using small, very flat buttons instead of tiddly wink disks.

You will need

a cardboard box (about 11 in. long, 8½ in. wide and ¾ in. deep)
a KnowHow circle maker (see page 5)
a paper cup
a ruler, a pencil and paint
strong glue and scissors
one big, flat button and 5 tiddly wink disks or small, flat buttons for each player

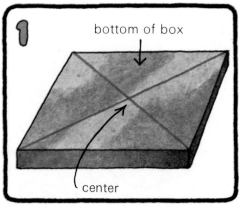

1

bottom of box

center

Find the center of the box by drawing lines across it from the four corners, like this. The center is where the lines cross.

2

center

4 in.

2½ in.

Draw a circle on the box, using the 4 in. hole of the circle maker. Draw a smaller circle, using a hole punched above the 2½ in. mark on the circle maker, like this.

3

(a)

glue paper cup

(b)

Cut the top off a paper cup so it is as deep as the box (a). Put the bottom of the cup in the center of the box. Draw around it. Cut out the circle. Glue the cup inside the hole (b).

4

Draw ten lines across the outside and inside circles to make ten sections, like this. Paint the sections different colors.

How to Play

Draw the numbers and words inside the sections. Each player has a big, flat button and five small tiddly winks. Players sit opposite each other, about 3 ft. from the board.

Taking turns, use the button to make the tiddly winks jump onto the board. The player with the highest score after all the tiddly winks have been jumped is the winner.

Skittle Scatter

(for 2 or more players)

You will need

8 cardboard tubes (each about 3 in. long)

a strong cardboard box without a lid (about 13 in. wide and 15 in. long)

a smaller box (about 12 in. wide and 12½ in. long)

thin cardboard, colored paper and aluminum foil

a big plate, a knitting needle, a hairpin and a thread spool

doweling (about 18 in. long) or a thin stick

strong glue and some string

a pencil, ruler and scissors

paint and a paintbrush

1 Making the Skittles

Paint the cardboard tubes. Leave them to dry. Paint on faces. Cut eight pieces of string, each about 32 in. long. Glue one end of each piece to the inside of each tube.

2

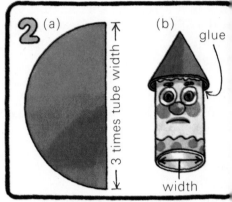

To make cone hats, cut out half-circles of thin cardboard at least three times as wide as the tubes (a. Roll them into cones and glue ther onto the tubes (b).

3

To make hair, cut slits in strips of thin paper about 14 in. long (a). Roll the paper up (b). Push a rolled strip into a cardboard tube and bend over the strips, like this (c).

4

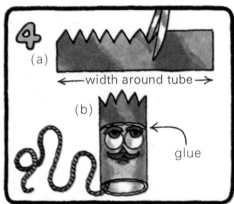

To make crowns, cut strips of thin cardboard, long enough to wrap around the tubes. Cut triangles on one edge of each strip (a). Wrap a strip around a tube and glue it (b).

5 Making the Base

Draw a circle on the bottom of the big cardboard box, close to one corner, using a big plate as a guide, like this.

6

Put strong glue around the edges of the smaller box. Glue it, bottom end up, to the inside of the big box, underneath the circle you have drawn. Let it dry.

7

Using a long knitting needle, make seven holes around the outside of the circle and one in the middle. Make sure the needle goes through the box glued under the circle.

8

Loop the string of one tube around hairpin (a). Push it through one of the holes and pull it out of the same hole in the box underneath (b). Do the same to all the tubes.

9

(a)

knot strings

(b)

make hole

Make a hole at both ends of the big box. Thread the four farthest strings from end (a) through that hole. Thread the other four strings through end (b), like this.

Pull all the strings, like this. Knot the four strings at either end together. When you pull the strings the skittles that have fallen over will stand up.

10 The Skittle Hitter

tie string

glue on thread spool

aluminum foil

To make the skittle hitter, glue a thread spool to the corner of the box. Wrap aluminum foil around the bottom of the stick and push it into the hole in the spool. Tie some string to the top of the stick. Tie a marble, wrapped in foil, to the other end, so it hangs just above the box, like this.

How to Play

Pull the strings to make all the skittles stand up. Swing the skittle hitter and try to knock over as many skittles as you can. Pull them up again. Each player has two swings in a turn. The first one to knock over 20 skittles is the winner.

Another way to play is to paint numbers, from 1 to 8, inside the skittles. To score, add up the numbers inside fallen skittles. The first to score 50 wins.

Cops and Robbers

(for 2 or 4 players)

This is a hunt through a maze. One player or team has six cops, the other has six robbers.

You will need
cardboard (about 18 in. long and 18 in. wide)
thin cardboard and tracing paper
modeling clay
2 paper cups
2 big buttons
thin elastic or thin rubber bands
white paper and strong glue
a pencil and a ruler
a red crayon and paint

Draw a square, 15 in. long and 15 in. wide, on the thick cardboard. Draw marks every 1¼ in. along the four sides of the square, like this (a).

Draw lines from the top marks to the bottom marks and from side to side to make small squares. Draw in the red lines as shown (b).

To make the hedges, roll pieces of clay into long strips, each about ¼ in. wide (a). Put the strips along the red lines drawn on the cardboard.

Push the clay strips down gently so that they stick to the cardboard. Then pinch the clay until the strips are about ¾ in. high, like this (b).

Make eleven clay tree shapes (a). Put them on top of the hedges, like this (b). Look at the big picture opposite to make sure you put the trees in the right places.

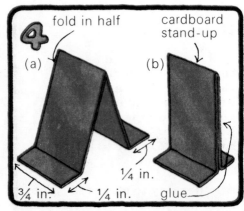

Cut out twelve strips of thin cardboard, each ¾ in. wide and 2¾ in. long. Fold them in half and bend out the ends (a). Glue the two halves together, like this (b).

Draw the cop pattern and the robber pattern (a) onto some tracing paper. Trace the cop pattern onto one side of six of the cardboard stand-ups.

Trace the robber pattern onto one side of the other six cardboard stand-ups. Then paint all the cops and robbers (b).

Cop Entrance

Robber Entrance

Robber Entrance

Cop Entrance

6

knot

¼ in.

button

bottom of cup

hole

(a)

(b)

cop gun

robber gun

Make a hole, ¼ in. from the base, on either side of the paper cups. Thread thin rubber bands through the holes and thread a big button onto the rubber bands. Knot the ends (a).

Cover the paper cups with white paper. Paint a picture of a cop on one of the cups and a picture of a robber on the other cup (b). These are the guns.

How to Play

The idea is to shoot all the other player's men. One player moves the cops and has the cop gun. The other moves the robbers and has the robber gun. If you play in teams of two, each player then moves three men.

To start, put three cops at each of the cop entrances and three robbers at each of the robber entrances. Each player moves one man 5 squares in a turn. They can move in any direction, except diagonally. To shoot an enemy, a player's man must land on the square next to one occupied by an enemy. He then pulls the button on his gun and shouts, "you are dead." He takes the man off the board.

Men can only jump over a hedge where there is a tree. They cannot shoot through a hedge except where there is a tree. The first player or team to shoot all of the enemy wins.

Picture Puzzles

(for 1 or more players)

Jumble up the Picture Box pieces. See who can put the picture in the right order in the shortest time.
Jumble up the Jigsaw pieces and make up the picture.
Tilt the Heads and Tails to get the balls into the holes. Shake it to get the rings on the pins.

For Picture Box you will need

a small, strong cardboard box
thin and thick cardboard
a picture or photograph
transparent tape and strong glue
scissors, a pencil and a ruler

1 Picture Box

(a) (b) same width (c) same length glue

Put the box onto a picture or photograph and draw around it (a). Cut the shape out, making it ⅛ in. smaller all the way around. Divide the length and width into three.

Draw lines across and down to make nine equal pieces, like this (b). Cut out the piece in the bottom right hand corner and glue it inside the box, as shown (c).

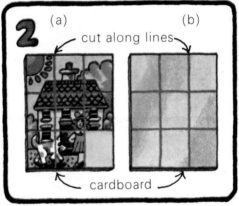

2 (a) cut along lines (b) cardboard

Cut two pieces of thin cardboard the size of the picture. Glue the picture to one piece (a) and cut along the lines. Divide the other piece into nine pieces (b). Cut along the lines.

3 thick cardboard same width same length

Cut a piece of thick cardboard half as big as the bottom of the box. Measure and draw lines across and down it to make nine equal pieces, like this. Cut along the lines.

4 picture piece plain piece ¼ in. thick piece ¼ in.

Glue a piece of thick cardboard in between a plain and a pictured piece, like this. The thick piece should stick out about ¼ in. from the left hand corner.

5 ⅛ in. ⅛ in.

Wait until the glue has dried on all eight sandwiched pieces. Then, using scissors, cut all the thick pieces into this shape.

6 cut slit tape ⅛ in. ⅛ in. cut slit

Cut a narrow slit on the bottom left side of the box and the front end, like this, without cutting through the corner. Put transparent tape over the corner, like this.

7

Put the picture into the right order. Then put the pieces into the box, like this, so that the thick pieces of cardboard slide inside the picture pieces on either side.

You will need

scissors, strong glue, a pencil
a ruler, paint or crayons

For the Jigsaw
thick cardboard
a picture or photograph

For the Heads and Tails
a round, deep cardboard
   box with a lid
thin cardboard
3 cake decoration balls (marbles)
a knitting needle
4 thumb tacks
4 small curtain rings
plastic wrap
2 pictures or photographs

1 Jigsaw   cut wriggly lines

Glue a picture onto some thick cardboard. Cut the cardboard in half in wriggly lines from top to bottom and from side to side, like this.

2

Cut the pieces in half again in wriggly lines. Go on cutting the pieces until you have lots of little pieces. Jumble them up and then make up the picture again.

1 Heads and Tails

lid of box —   bottom of box

draw around box

Draw two circles on some cardboard, using the bottom and the lid of the round box. Cut the circles out, making them a little smaller all the way around.

2   (a)   picture   knitting needle   (b)   (c)

cardboard   holes   glue inside box

Glue a picture or photograph to one circle (a). Make three holes in the picture using a knitting needle (b). Make sure the holes are free of any cardboard scraps.

See in which one it fits, and then glue the picture inside either the lid or the bottom of the box, like this (c).

3   (a)   picture   (b)   ½ in.   (c)

½ in.

cardboard   thumb tack points   glue inside box

Glue a picture or photograph to the other cardboard circle (a). Push four thumb tacks through the picture from underneath, like this (b), making sure they are not too close to the edges.

Glue the picture inside the other part of the box, like this (c). Let it dry.

4   plastic wrap   (a)

marbles   (b)   curtain rings   glue

Put the rings into the box with the thumb tacks and the balls into the other box. Glue plastic wrap to the tops of both boxes (a). When they dry, glue the lid to the bottom (b).

Shotpot
(for 2 or more players)

This is a shooting gallery. Try to shoot the buttons or beads out of the cups and down the ramp.

You will need
a cardboard box with a lid
  (about 12 in. x 6 in.)
6 paper cups of the same size
a sheet of cardboard
a piece of cloth
thick paper
a cannon (see page 17)
6 marbles and some beads or
  buttons
strong glue and transparent tape
a pencil and some scissors

1 Draw six circles inside the bottom of the cardboard box, using the bottom of a paper cup as a guide. Cut out the circles, making them a little smaller all the way around.

2 Make an opening, about 1¼ in. high and ¾ in. from each side, in one end of the cardboard box bottom. Cut along the red lines as shown.

3 Glue the cardboard box bottom about two-thirds of the way down the inside of the lid, like this. Cut out the bottoms of the paper cups.

4 Draw six circles on thick paper, using the bottom of a paper cup. Cut the circles out (a). Make a hole in the middle of each paper circle, using closed scissors.

Cut 12 slits from the hole to about ⅛ in. from the edge of each paper circle, like this (b). Glue one paper circle to the bottom of each paper cup (c). Let it dry.

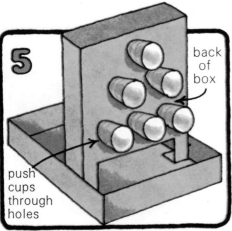

5 Push the cups, bottom end first, through the holes in the box, like this. The rims should just stick out on the other side.

6 Cut a strip of cardboard as wide as the inside of the box lid and about one-third of the length. Rest it on the back of the lid and tape it under the opening, like this.

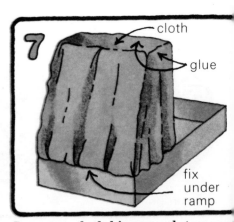

7 Cut some cloth big enough to cover the back and sides of the upright bo Glue one end of the cloth to the top the box. Put the other end under th cardboard ramp.

How to Play

Lift up the cloth and put three beads or buttons inside each paper cup. Fix the cloth under the ramp. Fire marbles from the cannon and try to knock the beads out of the paper cups, so they slide down the ramp and through the opening.

Each player fires six marbles in a turn. Each bead counts as one point. Add up the points after each turn. The first player to knock 20 beads through the opening wins.

glue on strip

cut open flap

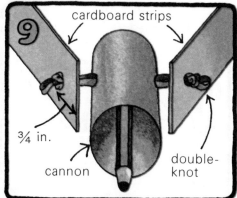

cardboard strips

¾ in.

cannon

double-knot

ut open the end of the box lid
d push it down flat. Cut two
rips of cardboard the same
ngth as the lid and as high.

Cut slits, about ¼ in. long, in one end of each cardboard strip. Bend the slits forward and glue them to the sides of the lid, like this.

Make a cannon (see page 17). Make a hole in both the cardboard strips, about ¾ in. from the ends. Push the two rubber bands through the holes and double knot the ends.

Floor War

(for 2 players or 2 teams)

You will need

an old bed sheet or cheap
  material (about 6½ ft. x 6½ ft.)
4 thumb tacks
tracing paper and white paper
thin cardboard and thin twigs
4 thread spools, 4 paper cups and
  4 cardboard 6-egg cartons
4 empty matchboxes, 4 short
  pencils and thick cardboard
strong rubber bands and lots of
  strips of paper
a ruler, a soft-tip pen and a pencil
scissors and paint
(You can also mark out the
squares of the battlefield with
chalk on any hard floor.)

1 The Battlefield (a)   (b)   marks
8 in.

thumb
tack
sheet

6 ft.

6 ft.

Pin the sheet or material to the floor
or carpet with thumb tacks, like this.
Draw a square, 6 ft. long and 6 ft.
wide, on the sheet or material using
a soft-tip pen (a).

Draw marks every 8 in. along the
sides of the square. Draw lines from
the top marks to the bottom marks
and from side to side, like this (b).

3 The Scenery
(b)

(a)

cup
covered
in paper

(c)

painted egg carton

twigs

thread
spool

Tree

House

Hill

To make a tree, push small twigs
into the hole in a spool (a). Wrap and
glue paper around a tall paper cup
and paint it, like this, to make a
house (b).

Cut an egg carton in half. Paint the
half with egg holders, like this, to
make hills (c). Make four trees, four
houses and four sets of hills.

4 Model Gun

glue on pencil

cardboard
wheels

To make a model gun, glue a sma[ll]
pencil or stick to the top of a
matchbox, like this. Glue two sm[all]
cardboard circles to each side. E[ach]
team needs two guns.

5 The Catapult
rubber
bands

(a) (b) (c)

bullet

catapult

paper
bullet

Link two rubber bands (a) to make
a catapult. Make paper bullets, as
shown (b). To fire, put a bullet
around the bands (c). Aim, pull back
the bullet and then let it go.

6 Setting Up
scenery

one
side's
soldiers

other
side's
soldiers

One side first lays out the scenery
in any way they like in the squares
on the battlefield. The other side
then chooses which edge they will
enter the field from.

The first side then enters from
the opposite edge. Each team sets
up its soldiers and guns in the
first row of squares at their edge
of the battlefield, like this.

2 The Soldiers

(a)

cavalry pattern (b)

glue

bend out

½ in.

infantry pattern

C

I

(c)

Cut out 20 strips of thin cardboard, each about 7 in. long and 1½ in. wide. Then cut out 40 smaller strips, each about 6 in. long and 1 in. wide. Fold the strips in half.

Bend out the ends, like this. Glue the two halves together (a). Trace the cavalry pattern on the 20 big stand-ups and the infantry pattern on the 40 smaller ones (b).

Draw a C on the back of the cavalry stand-ups and an I on the back of the infantry ones. Each team has 10 cavalry and 20 infantry. Paint each team's soldiers a different color (c).

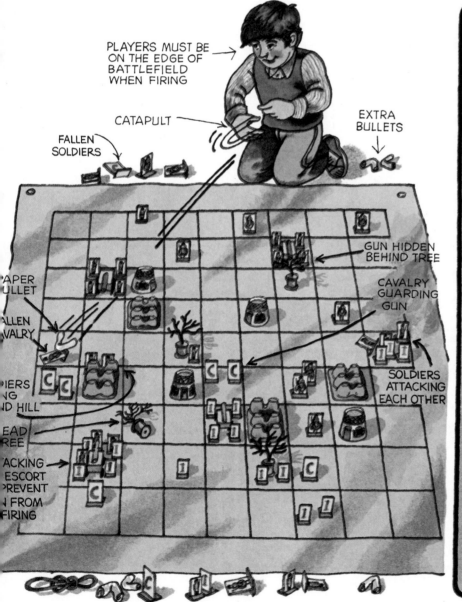

PLAYERS MUST BE ON THE EDGE OF BATTLEFIELD WHEN FIRING

CATAPULT

EXTRA BULLETS

FALLEN SOLDIERS

GUN HIDDEN BEHIND TREE

CAVALRY GUARDING GUN

SOLDIERS ATTACKING EACH OTHER

PAPER BULLET

FALLEN CAVALRY

SOLDIERS ... ND HILL

DEAD TREE

ATTACKING ... ESCORT ... PREVENT ... FROM FIRING

How to Play

The game is to put all enemy soldiers out of action. Each side has a catapult. Toss a coin to see which side starts. Both sides may move all their soldiers in a turn. Infantry, cavalry and guns can move in any direction except diagonally. Cavalry can move up to 3 squares in a turn. Infantry and guns only 1. Cavalry and guns cannot go into squares with scenery.

You must have 4 infantry in the same square as a gun for it to be allowed to move or fire. A gun can either move or fire once each turn. When a gun is within 6 squares of any enemy soldiers, use your catapult and paper bullets to knock them over. Fire from your side of the field over the model gun you are pretending to fire.

Take any soldiers knocked over by catapult fire off the field. As many soldiers as you like can occupy the same square, but the more there are the easier they will be to hit. Any soldiers put into the same square as enemy soldiers kill the same number of enemy soldiers, but also are killed themselves. The first side to put all the enemy soldiers out of action wins.

Space Mission

(for 2 or 3 players)

Play the game on this space board. There are twelve Galaxies, each with five stars.

You will need

3 red, 3 blue, 3 green spaceships
  (made as shown below)
1 white, 1 blue, 1 red die

How to Play

A player has three spaceships of one color, each with a white, blue or red flag. He moves his ships from Start to Finish, going from 1 Galaxy to 12 Galaxy in order. Each turn a player throws the three dice. He moves his ship with the white flag the number on the white die, the blue one for the blue die and the red one for the red die. Ships go in any direction along the lines, moving one red dot or star for each point on the dice. A player must have one ship on a Galaxy star before his other two can move to the next Galaxy. If a player throws the same number on all three dice, he has another turn. No ship can land twice on a dot or star in a turn. No ship can land on the same dot as another ship, or jump over a ship.

How to Score

Mark down your score after each turn. When a player's ship lands on a Galaxy star, it scores 1 point. If his second ship lands on a star while the first ship is on the same Galaxy, it scores 3 points. If his third ship lands on the same Galaxy, it scores 5 points.
The game ends when one player gets his three ships to Finish. Each ship scores 3 points when it reaches Finish. The player with the most points at the end of the game wins.

Make spaceships, like this. Glue on white, red or blue paper flags.

Party Games
(for lots of players)

Cotton Balls

Put two bowls beside each other on the floor. Fill one with cotton balls. Each player is blindfolded in turn and given a big spoon.

The idea is to scoop up the balls with the spoon and drop them into the empty bowl. Each player has three tries and scores 2 points for each ball he gets into the second bowl. The player with the most points at the end wins.

Murder in the Dark

Cut out as many slips of paper as there are players. Mark an X on one and a D on another. Leave the rest blank. Fold them in half and give one to each player. The player with the slip marked X is the murderer. He keeps it secret. D is the detective. He tells everyone.

The lights are put out and everybody hides except the detective. The murderer creeps up on a hidden player, whispers "you are dead" and runs off. The victim screams, the lights go on and everyone gathers around him. The detective asks questions to find out who the murderer is. Only the murderer can lie. The detective has 3 guesses to find the murderer.

Package Dressing Up

Wrap a bar of chocolate in layers of paper tied in string. Players sit in a circle with a hat, a scarf, gloves, glasses, a dull-bladed table knife and a fork in the middle. They take turns throwing dice. When someone throws a 6, he takes the clothes from the middle, puts them on and tries to open the package with the knife and fork.

The others go on throwing the dice. When one throws a 6, he pulls the clothes off the first person, puts them on and opens the package with the knife and fork. This goes on until the package has been opened and all the chocolate has been eaten.

The Mailing Game

Hide ten cans, each with the name of a city written on it, around the house. Each player gets a box with ten slips of folded paper in it. On each slip is written the name of one of the cities. All the boxes are put in one room.

Each player takes one slip at a time, writes his name on the back and rushes around the house to find the can with the same name as his slip. When he finds it, he places the slip in the can and goes back for his next slip. The first player to place all ten slips in the right cans is the winner.

Whisper Story

Everyone sits in a line. The player at one end makes up a long story and whispers it to the person beside him. The second player then whispers the story to the next person. This goes on down the line until the last person has heard the story. He tells it out loud. Then the first person tells the real story.

Sardines

One player hides somewhere in the house. He must hide in a place big enough to hold more people. The other players count to 50 and then go off to look for him. Anyone who finds him quietly joins him in the hiding place. The last person to find him loses.

Eaties

Everybody is blindfolded. A plate with ten different pieces of food on it is put in front of each player. They taste the food. The plates are taken away and the blindfolds taken off. The players write down what they think they have eaten. Put things like cold peas and cold potatoes on each plate.

Stop Game

Play this game while everyone is eating. First choose a "stop" caller. Everybody starts eating. Suddenly the caller shouts "stop" and everyone has to freeze. No one can eat or move, except the "stop" caller until he calls "move on." Everyone has a chance to be the "stop" caller.

Spin the Bottle

Put a bottle on a table and have everyone sit around the table. One player spins the bottle. Whoever it points to when it stops spinning has to pay a penalty. Think up lots of penalties before you begin, such as eating an apple without bending your elbows or chewing half a lemon.

Party Races
(for lots of players)

Stepping Stone Cans

Each player has two cans. They race each other from one end of the room to the other using their cans as stepping stones.

To start, stand on one foot on one can. Then bend down and, without touching the floor, put the second can in front of the first. Step on it with your other foot. Then bend down and put the first can in front. Do this again and again until you get to the other end of the room.

Flower Pot Stilts

To make a flower pot stilt, make a hole on each side of a plastic flower pot, near the base. Pull string through the holes and knot the ends.

Players split into two teams. Each team has two stilts. They stand at one end of the room with two chairs at the other. The first player in each team stands on the stilts, holds the string, walks around the chair and back and gives the stilts to the next player. The first team to get around the chair and back wins.

Orange Under the Chin

Two teams stand in two lines. The first player in each team puts an orange under his chin.

The game is to pass the orange from chin to chin down your line without touching it with your hands. If a player drops or touches it, the orange must go back to the beginning of his line. The first team to get its orange to the end of the line wins.

Peas and Straws

Each player has a straw, 30 dried peas in a cup and an empty cup. He puts the cups next to one another on the floor. He has to suck the peas onto the end of his straw and drop them into the empty cup. The first player to get all his peas into the second cup is the winner.

Peas and Pull-Boxes

To make a pull-box, make two holes about 6 in. apart, in one end of a box. Pull string through the holes and knot the ends.

Players split into two teams and stand at one end of the room with a line of string at the other. Each team has a pull-box with 40 dried peas lined up in front of it. Each member of the team has to pull the box, without losing the peas, to the line and back. The team with the most peas left in front of its box after all the players have pulled it wins.

String Rolls

[Ti]e string across a room, about 6 ft. from the floor. [C]ut as many 3 ft. pieces of string as there are [pl]ayers. Tie one end of each piece to the string [a]cross the room. Thread the other end of each [pi]ece through a roll. Knot the ends.

[Ea]ch player has to eat a roll without touching it [w]ith his hands. The first to eat his roll wins.

Matchbox Noses

[T]wo teams stand in two lines. The first player [in] each team puts a matchbox cover on his nose.

[T]he game is to pass the matchbox from nose to nose [d]own your line, without touching it with your [h]ands. If a player drops or touches it, the matchbox [m]ust go back to the beginning of his line. The first [te]am to get its matchbox to the end of the line wins.

Tissue Fish

[Ea]ch player gets a rolled up newspaper, and a [fis]h shape cut out of tissue paper. Players split into [tw]o teams and stand at one end of the room with [tw]o big plates at the other end.

[Th]e first player in each team puts his fish on the [flo]or and flaps the newspaper behind it until he [ge]ts the fish into his plate. As soon as he does, the [ne]xt player in his team starts. The first team to [ge]t all its fish into its plate wins.

Tissue Squares

Cut out as many squares of tissue paper as there are players. Put two pillows at one end of the room and two plates at the other. Lie half the number of tissue squares on one pillow and half on the other. Players split into two teams. Each team stands next to a plate.

The first player in each team has a spoon. He runs to the pillow, scoops up a tissue square with the spoon, without touching it, and carries it back to his plate. If he drops it, he must scoop it up again without touching it. Once it is on the plate the next player starts. The first team to get all its squares onto its plate wins.

Balloon Bursting

Players split into two teams. They stand at one end of the room. Two chairs, each heaped with as many balloons as there are players in a team, are at the other end.

The first player in each team runs to the chair, blows up a balloon, knots it and sits on it until it bursts. He runs back and touches the next player, who runs to the chair. The first team to blow up and burst all its balloons wins.

45

Treasure Hunts

(for lots of players)

Arrange the treasure hunts before the party begins. Try not to hide any clues in dangerous places and make sure that even the smallest player can reach them. Tell everyone which rooms are not being used in the hunt.

Players can either hunt by themselves, in pairs or teams.

In a clue-by-clue hunt, try not to let anyone else know that you have found a clue. When you have read it make sure you put it back where you found it.

Camouflage Hunts

Hide 20 small, colored things, like a red pencil, a yellow button or a green toothbrush, around the house. Hide each thing in or on something of the same color, perhaps the yellow button on a yellow book or the green toothbrush on a green plate.

Each player gets a list of the hidden things and a pencil and starts looking. When he finds one he writes down its hiding place. The first player to write down the hiding places of all 20 things wins.

Clue-by-Clue Hunts

Write the clues on pieces of paper. Hide them around the house, say in a shoe or faucet. Each clue tells the players where to find the next clue until they reach the treasure.

Read out the first clue to all th[e] players. In this hunt, the fir[st] clue is: "You'll find clue no. 2 [if] you put your foot in me." No[w] follow the clues to find the treasure.

TO FIND THE NEXT *CLUE* – PICK ME UP AND SPEAK TO ME...

AS YOU SLEE[P] I GET FLATTE[R] AND FLATTE[R] – LOOK UNDE[R] ME FOR TH[E] NEXT *CLUE*

YOU OFTEN STAND ON ME – LOOK UNDER ME FOR THE NEXT *CLUE*...

USE ME TO UNTANGLE THE NEXT *CLUE*...

I LOO[K] AND S[] GOOD – IN ME [] THE N[] CL[]

THE NEXT *CLUE* GETTING COLD[] AND COLDER–F[] BEFORE IT FRE[]

Hidden Letters

Hide the treasure, say in the bathroom. Write the letters that spell "bathroom" on different pieces of paper. Hide them. Tell everyone how many letters are hidden.

As they find one, the players write down each letter. When a player thinks he knows which room the letters spell, he runs to that room to find the treasure.

THINGS HANG IN ME. I'M OFTEN UNTIDY— SEARCH ME FOR THE TREASURE...

ANSWER THE TREASURE IS HIDDEN IN THE CUPBOARD

SWITCH ME ON TO FIND THE NEXT *CLUE*...

Hidden Pictures

Cut some magazine pictures or old Christmas cards in half. Give one half of each picture to a player and hide the other halves around the house.

The first player to find the hidden half of his picture gets a prize. You can make it more difficult by cutting the pictures into quarters and hiding three pieces.

THE NEXT *CLUE* WILL COME SPLASHING OUT IF YOU TURN ME ON...

Scavenger Hunts

Each player gets a list of the same ten things to find, perhaps a shoe, a nail, a potato or a hairpin. All the things are somewhere in the house. A player has to collect one of each thing on his list in a certain time, perhaps 15 minutes.

The player who has collected the most things on his list at the end of the time limit is the winner.

Left Standing

Players are shown a small object. They go out of the room. The object is hidden so only a little of it shows. Everyone comes back into the room and starts looking for it.

When a player sees it he sits down. He does not tell anyone he has seen it or where it is. The last person to see it is left wandering around the room on his own.

Index

animals of four, 26
balloon bursting, 45
battleships, 27
beetle bugs, 6
blow football, 13
camouflage hunts, 46
cannon, 17
cannonboard, 16-17
cardboard dice, 5
catapult, 38
catchball, 12
circle maker, 5
clay dice, 5
clue-by-clue hunts, 46-47
cops and robbers, 32-33
cotton balls, 42
crossing the line, 23
dice, 5
drawing blind, 27
eaties, 43
egg flip, 12
finding the middle, 5
five minute games, 12-13
fish hook, 15
fish making, 15
flick billiards, 18
floor war, 38-39
flower pot stilts, 44
frog leaps, 7
getting ready, 4
grand derby, 22
hangman, 26
heads and tails, 35
hidden letters, 46
hidden pictures, 47
homemade boxes, 4
hop over, 25
jigsaw, 35
jockey, 22
jumbled newspapers, 26
jumpers, 29
keep on folding, 27
knowhow circle maker, 5
knowhow timer, 15
left standing, 47
looping the loop, 10-11

matchbox bullseye, 13
matchbox noses, 45
matchmake, 24
materials, 4
model gun, 38
mouse trap, 14
murder in the dark, 42
noise maker, 26
orange under the chin, 44
paper games, 26-27
paper hats, 26
parcel dressing up, 42
party games, 42-43
party races, 44-45
peas and pull-boxes, 44
peas and straws, 44
picture box, 34
picture puzzles, 34-35
posting game, 42
push and shove, 28
ribbon roll, 13
sardines, 43
scavenger hunts, 47
scenery, 38
shotpot, 36-37
skittle scatter, 30-31
soldiers, 39
space mission, 40-41
spinner, 14
spin the bottle, 43
stepping stone cans, 44
sticks and kicks, 20-21
stop game, 43
string rolls, 45
sugar dice, 5
team drawing, 26
there and back, 8-9
tiddly pong, 19
timer, 15
tissue fish, 45
tissue squares, 45
treasure hunts, 46-47
2-in-1 board, 24-25
whisper story, 43
who begins?, 4